THE MECHANICS OF GRATITUDE

CHRIS PALMORE

Cover Design: Nathaniel Dasco

Back Cover Photo: Corey Boston

All Artwork In This Book By Anthony Lee Lowe

Copyright © 2021 by Chris Palmore

All rights reserved.

No part of this book may be reproduced in any form or by any electronic or mechanical means, including information storage and retrieval systems, without written permission from the author, except for the use of brief quotations in a book review.

To this present moment,

Now,

To your full potential...

To the spectrum of emotions that you cover...

I'm grateful for your valuable gift of life.

I'm grateful for the memory of you, on which I can reflect later.

You and every gift and lesson you bring me are precious.

I am fortunate to have you and to be here with you.

In gratitude...

Chris

CONTENTS

Foreword 7
Introduction 11

1. Podcast 13
2. Monastery 17
3. Campaign 21
4. Choice 23
5. Anniversary 27
6. Perspective 31
7. Focus 35
8. Gratitude 39
9. Definition 43
10. Practice 47
11. Mindfulness 51
12. Contagious 55
13. Hope 59
14. Encounters 63
15. Roadmap 67
16. Reflexive 69
17. Intentional 73
18. Emotion 77
19. Relation 81
20. Catalyzing 85
21. Mindset 91

For Further Study 93
Gratitude Checklist 95
About the Author 97
Also by Chris Palmore 99

FOREWORD

Paul S. Boynton is the author of several books, including bestsellers Begin with Yes *and* Be Amazing.

I first want to take this opportunity to thank the "Begin with Yes" community of over 2.3 million positive people that motivate and inspire me daily. I also want to thank Chris for giving me the opportunity to write this foreword.

I was honored when Chris asked me to write the foreword for this book. It seems like only yesterday that we met. In reality, as I reflect back, it's been almost six years. I remember him first reaching out, wanting to feature me on his GratitudeSpace website, and because I practice what I preach, I began with YES!

I remember him asking me to answer a series of questions he referred to as *grati-questions*. The first question was what being grateful meant to me. I provided a long answer and finished with one additional thought, "Being grateful is both a feeling we have and an expression we make. Feeling grateful is wonderful, and expressing it by helping others is even better!"

It's for this one reason that I am now gratefully writing this foreword.

In my opinion, gratitude is all about remembering what you are grateful for and finding a way to express it. I was surprised to see how far Chris has come on his own gratitude journey and blown away to see how he is now providing a framework for others to explore their own gratitude. I believe that this book falls in line with the elements I have been teaching in my own books: finding new ways to experience joy in life. In this, Chris and I are on similar paths.

As I get older, I continue to be both surprised and happy when I discover something new or learn how to do something better. Most things in our lives are based on trial and error, and fortunately, there are teachers everywhere we look. Life can be its own teacher. Thinking of gratitude as a skill, something we can learn, like going to the gym, is a revolutionary idea. Science has proven that one's health is related to one's gratitude. What would my gratitude fitness routine be? How would I get my reps in today? Roy T. Bennett says, "Grateful people are happy people. The more things you are grateful for, the happier you will be." What would it be like to live this quote?

To quote Meerabelle Dey, "We have to turn the concept of gratitude from a noun into a verb." *The Mechanics of Gratitude* turns a gratitude practice into actionable steps to remember, feel, and ultimately experience the true magic and power of gratitude.

In this book, Chris Palmore has created a five-step process for waking out of a reflective state and moving into an intentional, relational, emotional one, providing a guide for anyone to practice gratitude, taking single non-emotional elements and tagging them with memories and moments that bring out the power and magic that lives inside a grateful heart.

The potential benefits include recovering from depression, hopelessness, and ingratitude to being present and ultimately feeling that this moment is enough, that we are enough! Keep shining the light and fanning the flames of gratefulness, as we continue to *catalyze* gratitude!

I think Goethe had it right when he said, "Knowing is not enough; we must apply. Willing is not enough; we must do." This book will move people from knowing to applying to doing.

Continue to be amazing!

Paul S. Boynton

INTRODUCTION

My gratitude journey began when I experienced a tremendous loss about eight years ago. That was the beginning of a long period of reflection and self-exploration for me, one that led me to a new path — that of pursuing gratitude. I want to share my journey and all the discoveries I made along the way. My hope is that sharing my findings will allow readers to see their lives in a whole new light.

1

PODCAST

It all started in 2013 when I accompanied my friend Corey from Louisville, Kentucky, to his new home in San Francisco, California, to help him relocate. One night, we went to a comedy club to see Adam Carolla do his stand-up routine. With humility and humor, Adam shared his story. He also mentioned his podcast, The Adam Carolla Show.

Back in Kentucky, I started listening to Adam's podcast regularly. In one of his sessions, he said he didn't celebrate his birthday because he felt that a birthday was life's version of a participation trophy. That made me think about my birthday, which was coming up. I may have only participated in my birth, but my mother hadn't; she had gone through childbirth. I decided to find a way to celebrate my mother on my birthday.

On December 30th, 2013, my 35th birthday, with the intention of both surprising my mom and making it public, I posted a message on her Facebook wall.

December 30th, 2013 - My 35th Birthday

Dear Mom,

I turned 35 today and this question has been floating around in my head the last few days: I'm all for celebrating with others, don't get me wrong, but could there be a better way to celebrate my birthday?

If I'm being totally honest with you, I didn't really do anything on December 30th, 35 years ago. I truly have no memory of it.

Now if you ask my mom, I'm sure she could tell you and convey a strong emotion with the events leading up to and including my birth. Is this day mine, really, to celebrate? Is living out another 365 days worth celebrating?

I'm not suggesting not celebrating the day of your birth, I'm suggesting that you celebrate your mom on your birthday. There are many reasons for this train of thought. Here are two: first, we have no memory or any true action on our part surrounding the event; second, as much as we enjoy receiving gratitude, giving true gratitude is a much healthier and fulfilling action.

I have no problem admitting that I'm selfish. I believe that there are selfish acts that a person can perform that are truly wonderful. When thanking someone, the giver is the one that benefits. I'd like to repeat that.

When being kind to another, the giver is the one that truly benefits. You can't feel what the other person is feeling. What you feel is the vibe you get from how you make them feel.

Now I know that I'm not the first person to think of this. I just wanted to tell my mom that I love her, that I appreciate the pain, suffering, and self-sacrifice she has endured on my behalf not only on the day of my birth but also for the years that followed, that I am fully aware that I wasn't always the easiest person to love, but she always made me feel loved. I just wanted to tell her all this on my birthday.

Mom, I pledge this coming year to tell you that I love you more often, and I will find more ways to let you know how special you are to me and make you prouder.

Love always,

Chris

That morning, my parents didn't call as they normally did on my birthday. I couldn't wait to find out my mother's reaction to the message, so a couple hours later, I called my dad, who answered with a musical *happy birthday*. After a quick chat, I asked him if he knew whether or not Mom had seen the message I had posted. He said she had, "She was so moved by it that she needed time to process it all. She was speechless."

My mom and I had always been close, so having made her speechless blew me away. I had adjusted the privacy setting of the Facebook post to public, so a large number of people commented on it and shared it. My appreciation for my mom on my birthday made a splash, and others were expressing their own appreciation for their loved ones. Gratitude breeds gratitude. At the time, I didn't know that her cancer would come back and four months to the day later, on April 30th, take her away.

The week after my mom's death, my thoughts kept circling around what I had written to her — that I would tell her I love her more this year and spend more time with her. Knowing I didn't have the opportunity to do all I had promised made sadness and depression take over. My despair didn't allow any light into this darkness.

My cousin read my Facebook message at her funeral, and, eventually, many friends and relatives wrote their own letters to my late mother, expressing their thoughts, feelings, and memories.

It took a while, but once I gradually regained the ability to focus, I realized my expression of gratitude had strengthened our bond during the last four months of my mother's life, and we had grown even closer than before. I felt grateful for having had the idea to write that message. It had come from Adam Carolla, and I felt grateful for him.

As time passed, my thoughts evolved around finding ways to encourage others to express their gratitude to their loved ones, have a beautiful experience, and feel all the love I had felt. I just didn't know how to do that, so I asked a few friends to write gratitude letters on their birthdays.

2

MONASTERY

I needed to get away from everything for a while and concentrate on my life, my new life with a giant hole in it. I looked for cabins in remote areas, but every place I found cost too much. Thankfully, a friend mentioned a monastery located in Kentucky. A quick search online revealed the Abbey of Gethsemani in Bardstown. Only an hour away, this hundred-year-old place hosted individuals in exchange for a donation. I contacted a monk to get more information: When could I go and how long could I stay?

Excited about a weekend adventure into solitude in a holy place, I woke up early on the day I was set to travel and drove there despite the blizzard — very unusual for Kentucky. When I arrived, I felt overwhelmed: Everything was quiet all around, a vast expanse all draped in white snow and no one to be found. I made my way inside the building and rang a little bell. A kindly monk appeared, explained the rules, and showed me to my room — a spacious room with bare brick walls and a private bathroom.

After a chat with the monk, I decided this was going to be a silent retreat for me. The place was quiet and eerily peaceful, just what I needed to meditate and reflect. I learned the necessary schedules for food and service, got settled, and found a spot where I had a bird's eye view of the hillside and the forest that were blanketed in white. I felt a part of it all but from a distance and there was no one else up there.

The next morning, I was sitting in my bed when a sound notified me of a message: Kate, my best friend's wife, had written a letter of gratitude to her parents on her birthday. I took a breath and read it.

Thinking of You on My Birthday

Dear Mom and Dad,

Happy birthday to me! Woohoo! I made it to 30! That thought makes me smile, grimace and shudder simultaneously. I am making a conscious effort not to grimace too much, however, as wrinkles are not something I just read about in books anymore. These well-earned lines on my face convey I've been here for a little while now and I've experienced a great deal of excitement! I've often been told I don't have a good poker face. 30. Thirty. THərdē/. I am thirty, happy and healthy. I have terrific friends who remain constant despite miles of distance between us. My wonderful, adventurous husband keeps life's remarkable wheels spinning wildly beneath my feet, and yet always catches me when I get tripped up. My energetic, animated daughter has taught me to love more deeply and passionately than I ever imagined possible. And I have a crazy, snarly puppy that would give his left nut for just 5 minutes of playing fetch.

How did I get here, to this point? Well we most certainly need not get into the nitty gritty details, but I am immensely grateful that you two loved each other so very much on that special night about 30 years and 10 months ago – give or take. If it weren't for that precise moment there would be no ME! That, however, is only a mere speckle of the story. Nature + nurture. So I was born and then you raised me. Mom, you taught me to be strong and independent, to stand tall with my shoulders back (or else you would dig your freaking knuckles into my spinal column)! Dad, you taught me how to think outside of the box, how to resolve puzzles when pieces are missing, and how to "MacGyver" anything. Your mutual support of my endeavors in school, athletics, and my career is something I cherish always and will excitedly pass on to my children. You taught me that my best is always good enough. Your empowering trust has driven me to work hard and give my all in life. My life is great because of this, because of you.

You raised me to be tough, to laugh, to tell a joke and to take a joke. You taught me sarcasm in all its glory. You taught me how to fight, and then how to apologize and forgive. You taught me to respect my elders and be kind to my neighbors. You taught me to be honest and just. You taught the good and the bad. You showed me life in its most beautiful, vulnerable and dreadful states. You welcomed sick relatives in to live with us, knowing they would breathe their last breaths in our home. You comforted and cared for them during their last days, helping them find peace in those trying moments. Through these and your multitude of selfless actions over the years, you taught me empathy and understanding, generosity and compassion. You taught me to feel sadness and despair, and to grow through these raw emotions. You taught me to be grateful for my life and all that I have in this moment. You taught me to truly live, to feel alive. No matter how challenging some moments may seem, I know how to find the good in life and that it is never too far away. You taught me this. I am so very lucky to be alive... to be 30... to be your daughter. I love you two more than you will ever know because words and actions cannot display my heart's story. I am thankful for you always. I am proud to call you Mom and Dad and I will do the best I can in life. I hope this proves you did the best you could raising me.

Thanks for giving me thirty birthdays. I look forward to thirty-one.

I love you,

Katie Kates

It was beautiful and I was crying. But I wasn't crying because it was beautiful... I knew that feeling and it wasn't this. This was a new feeling entirely. I didn't know what was happening. I was crying, completely caught up in an emotion, and I didn't know what it was.

What was happening to me? After searching myself for some time, I figured out what was happening. This letter I was reading on my computer, this letter of love, appreciation, and gratitude, existed in the physical world because I'd asked Kate to write it. Kate had these feelings inside of her. She expressed herself by writing them down, and all I had done was ask her to write a letter and share it with me... and the world.

This changed my life. I have never been the same since. I was forever transformed, having known the power of asking another to share love in this form that can be shared and viewed by all.

3

CAMPAIGN

I asked someone to share gratitude for another, and it sparked love and allowed gratitude to flow and multiply. The magic in this can be sensed only with complete presence and awareness. This brought me into the moment and gave me the opportunity to appreciate my life. This magic has a power that can turn famine into feast and darkness into light. It makes this moment enough.

Ever since my mom's passing, I wanted others to feel the love I had felt by expressing my gratitude to her on my birthday. Maybe simply asking others to share their gratitude, birthday or not, was the answer? I still had to work on the logistics. I set up a website and looked for new ways to encourage people to write letters.

One of the first ideas I had was to ask friends to write letters of appreciation to one individual. I then collected a week's worth of letters, and that person would receive these gratitude letters every day for a week. I did this several times. I surprised people by sending them letter after letter, from the collection I had received, for a week. The person would check their email or Facebook and see the letter was there to click on and read. This worked well, and the people who participated then continued to share love for others. It formed a circle of letter-writing love. With the help of the letters' authors, I did a week for my grandma, one for my sister, one for each of my mom's best friends, one for my mom's cancer doctor, and so forth.

One of my sister's good friends, Amy, had been going to cancer treatments for months, and I decided I would start two campaigns for her, one letter and one video. I traveled to her former workplace and gathered gratitude videos from her friends. Also, my sister had a big gathering at her cabin, and I collected more videos there. I had lots of letters come in from some of the people in the videos, too. In the end, I arranged two full weeks of letters and videos. I posted these love notes and videos so that she would get them when she was clear across the country, away from her family and friends, receiving treatments for her cancer.

I wanted to spread this idea of letter writing among more people and make these expressions of appreciation more popular. I also wanted people to see how much they had to be thankful for — and not just for other people but things too. I didn't know how to make people see. All I could do was share my own story. Maybe if they heard it, really heard it, they would wake up and appreciate every second with their own loved ones? It was easier said than done, though. People couldn't see it or get it, not without the right state of mind and the right perspective.

4

CHOICE

Perspective is everything. It determines our unique way of interpreting the events around us and reacting to them.

In *The Life-Changing Power of Gratitude*, Marc Reklau shares a parable about twin brothers whose father was a raging alcoholic. After a childhood filled with inconceivable abuse, one of the two brothers becomes a successful businessman, loved throughout their town because of his kindness and generosity, whereas the other follows in his father's footsteps and abuses everyone who crosses his path. The father dies. One day, the family doctor is called on to check up on the businessman. The doctor, who hasn't seen him in years, asks him how he became so successful. The businessman replies, "Doctor you know how... You knew my father."

Months later, the doctor visits the twin brother and notices the miserable way he lives and feels the anger and negative vibes in the air. The doctor looks at the man and asks him why he and his house are in such bad shape. The twin replies, "Doctor you know how... You knew my father."

Any two people, even twins, can have the same experience and choose to react in different ways based on how they look at it. At any given moment, we get to decide what each experience means to us and how it affects us. We decide if we are the first brother or the second brother, a hero or a victim, just as my friend Deano Sutter said on my podcast.

Michael O'Brien, author of *Shift: Creating Better Tomorrows: Winning at Work and in Life*, contributed a personal story on perspective, titled "I Think They Look Cool, Dad" to *Dear Gratitude: An Anthology*, a book I published in 2020. In it, he recounts his daughter's reaction to his skin grafts — she thought they looked cool. He writes, "Since my near-death cycling accident in 2001 that necessitated my skin grafts, I hated my scars. All I wanted to do was to cover them up because I thought everyone was staring at them. Many did, but I thought they looked at me with pity rather than strength. But when she thought they were cool, something shifted within me. Kids can be brutally honest, and her perspective gave me a moment to see them differently. It made me wonder, could I see my scars as marks of resilience rather than imperfection? So slowly, I started to see my scars through a lens of gratitude. They weren't ugly; they were merit badges that showed I survived something horrific. They were my indication that I was still alive."

Today, he sees his body, mind, and soul as Kintsugi art, a Japanese art form — a process where the artist mends broken pottery and mends it with gold, silver, or platinum, producing beautiful scar lines.

Our body is a gift. Taking care of our health and our body is a form of gratitude.

My friend Ifumi Ehigiator, a Nigerian writer and poet, author of *Age of the Sun*, writes about how dealing with challenging flaws led to self-love.

After escaping drowning in that sea of low self-esteem, I realized nothing makes anyone else better than me. Rather, we are all unique beings. Despite being mocked, I moved on and gradually began to struggle towards self-consciousness and self-love. There were those sincere enough to admire unique traits of mine. This proved to me that everyone is a two-sided coin. They have flaws and admirable traits alike. No one deserves to be humiliated. Self-love and self-consciousness, when in abundance, can positively impact life, all-round, and can also promote productivity.

Nobody's perfect. We all have mental and physical flaws. It's important to recognize – and be grateful for – what we can feel and everything we're capable of doing. Appreciating, loving, and respecting our *self* allows us to appreciate, love, and respect others and connect with them.

5

ANNIVERSARY

For the first anniversary of my mom's passing, I asked friends and relatives to write letters of love to my mom and share memorable events. I myself got up early and went to Starbucks to work on the website I was creating for my gratitude project. I posted a new letter of love people had written for my mom every hour for fifteen hours. That day, sitting at our favorite lunch place, I wrote my own letter to her.

Mommy,

Where to start... It's been an eventful year since you've been gone.

I've had to really get in touch with living a life where I can't talk with you every day. I miss your voice. I miss the way you would sneeze. You sounded like a little Tweety bird and I miss it. I miss our walks and how you made me feel like the most special person in the entire world.

I'd like to let you know that Dad and I are spending a lot more time together. I moved in with him out in Shelbyville six or so weeks ago and we are now not only father and son but roommates. This arrangement is perfect! Well, almost perfect. We both have a big piece missing from our lives which is you. I know that even if I get to live a long life nothing will ever fill the space that is me missing you.

I think that you would be proud of me. I've internalized the truth that we all have the choice of what we want to focus on. I daily think of you and when I get sad in these moments I make a choice of how long I want to be in that moment. I think of what you would want and if it's a sad moment I redirect. I'm having to stay in this place a little longer right now to write this.

Right now, I'm at our sushi restaurant, Kansai. I'm having a Derby Roll in your honor. I wish you were here to share this moment with me. I remember the last time I was here before you passed. I brought a Derby Roll home for you. You couldn't eat it because of the medication. I ended up eating it.

You sure did leave some big shoes to fill. I've been doing my best to shine the light of gratitude that you have left in me on the world. I foresee millions of people sharing gratitude throughout the entire world because of your love. There is a huge wave of gratitude coming; it's going to wipe some of the negativity and hate out of the world. This will be happening because you chose to love me. I love you so much, Mom.

Your Forever Grateful Son, Chris

I felt I had created a powerful way to celebrate my mom and her passing. All these wonderful people had taken the time to write a letter to someone no longer alive, shared their love, and expressed gratitude. The truth is that with love there will always be loss. If we love someone, we will be sad if we outlive them. All we can do is take the good memories and be grateful for having them, for having the time and the experience of loving another person. The amazing thing about love is that it can go on. If someone you know dies, you can continue to love them. I continue to love my mom when I think of her and her love for me.

6

PERSPECTIVE

I wasn't the only one who had outlived my mother. My dad, my sister, and I had all been coping with our new state, each in our own way. Watching my father deal with the death of the love of his life had jolted me out of my self-pity and reminded me I wasn't the only one grieving. Interacting with my father and sister allowed me to see their new world without mom, experience new perspectives, and learn to empathize.

As much as my sister and I were struggling with our loss, I could see my dad had gotten the worst of it. He didn't know what to do with himself in the house he had shared with my mother. Every inch of the house must have been a painful reminder of her absence because he sold what was my mom's dream house and moved out just to be able to breathe again.

Over a year later, even though he had moved, he didn't seem to be getting better accustomed to life without her. My sister thought getting him a pet might help, so she brought him a dog, but my dad wasn't ready for a companion. He just wanted to be alone, so he returned the dog. We tried again later, this time with a cat, a few months before the second anniversary of my mother's death, hoping he would accept it and it would help him get out of his miserable state of total sadness.

Years later, in 2020, my dad contributed to the anthology I was working on and submitted a piece titled "My Kitty Cat Gracie Jean" to be considered for *Dear Gratitude*. In it, he wrote:

Gracie is a wonderful friend to me. I hope I am one for her. I am forever grateful that God brought this amazing, sweet, sensitive, kind, warm, and fuzzy creature into my life. The joy that she brings has helped me to take on life. Just knowing that she gets excited to see me pull up in the driveway and how she greets me at my front door makes it a little easier to come home.

"Animals are a gift from above for they truly define the words unconditional love." Heather Wolf

This reminds me of my cat, Boog. She was sweet and loving. She would come and rub up against my leg and she would sleep with me, cradled in my arm with her head on my shoulder.

Her name comes from when she was a baby. We had adopted her from the humane society. After she was with us for a week or two, she developed this wicked sinus infection. It was so bad that snot would block her nose and make it hard for her to breathe. Fortunately, the medicine the vet prescribed cleared it up. Because of this, she was always affectionately nicknamed Boog. I'm grateful for the time I had with Boog. Remembering these moments allows me to appreciate her more even though she is no longer with me.

Pets really are good teachers. They teach us to be present in the moment, to appreciate our now, to practice mindfulness. Some research has also shown having a pet is the best form of self-care.

7

FOCUS

On the second anniversary of my mom's passing, I hosted Gratitude New York. I still didn't know exactly what I was doing. All I knew was I wanted more people to get the feeling I had when I realized tolerating my mother's passing would have been so much harder if I hadn't sent her that message on my birthday. It was as if I considered myself lucky that I got to share that with her. There was a sense of joy and satisfaction despite all the sadness. What is the opposite of regret? That was the feeling I wanted everyone to have.

In New York City, I was walking around one early morning and met two African American men in their late fifties near Times Square — Joe and Carl. I'm not sure how we initiated our conversation. I think they asked for money because I distinctly remember asking them what they really wanted. Carl said he wanted some new shoes, which unfortunately I couldn't give him because I didn't have enough money. I offered to buy them coffee or a sandwich from a nearby McDonald's and we headed toward it. I found out that Carl had just been released from prison that same day and Joe had planned to take him to his apartment, but his live-in girlfriend wouldn't let him. That's how they had ended up walking the streets in the middle of the night.

During breakfast, we talked about gratitude and being thankful. Carl felt he didn't have much to be grateful for until I reminded him he wasn't in prison anymore. He then laughed and admitted he hadn't looked at his situation that way. The disappointment of now being homeless had blinded him so much he couldn't see and appreciate that he was free.

After we parted, I thought about my own life and realized how fortunate I had been and how often I had forgotten that. It's easy to put aside all that's good and focus on what we consider problems. It's easy to forget how fortunate we are — all of us who have been given the gift of life. We have already won the lottery of life. Every single day is a gift, made of hours and minutes and seconds, each of which matter. How we choose to look at each gift and how we choose to spend each of these is important, mostly to us. When we see these as gifts, the tone for our next thought and action is set.

Loss and grief had often messed with my own appreciation for the many seconds, minutes, hours, days, weeks, and months that followed my mother's death, and, even in a state of gratitude, I had allowed my focus to be on the precious presence that was lacking in my life instead of the gift of life itself.

"It's a funny thing about life, once you begin to take note of the things you are grateful for, you begin to lose sight of the things that you lack." Germany Kent

I look at every day of my life as a gift and try to make the most of each, even those difficult days. One recurring challenge is each anniversary of my mother's passing. I've learned to be in my *now* and honor my mother by sharing more and more gratitude. Every year, I try to do better than the previous year. This year, I published the first volume of my journal, Gratitude Journey, on the anniversary of my mother's death.

It's not only about anniversaries, though. Every moment of every day is precious. I try to create little reminders of happiness. It's all about the little things, those little signals that redirect us to our present moment. It's important to have those little reminders. Every person may have a different one. For some, it might be an object that has a sentimental value; for many, it's their morning cup of coffee; and for animal lovers, it's a companion. In my present moment, I appreciate being healthy, loved, and actively in pursuit of my dreams. I'm grateful… but what does it really mean to be grateful?

8

GRATITUDE

If I was going to pursue a journey of gratitude, the first step was to know, really understand, the meaning of gratitude. The dictionaries I consulted all had the same definitions such as appreciation and thankfulness, but like most abstract words, it could easily vary in definition from one individual to the next and even be misunderstood.

The best way to get the meaning of the word was to ask people. I started asking people what gratitude meant to them — something I still do, just to see how others define it, even though I now have a clear understanding of it. I recently started a #GratitudeIs campaign to get more and more ideas of how others perceive it. I have a large collection of what gratitude means to others:

Gratitude Is:

"positivity which makes one see, learn, thank and encourage all the good in others" by Ravindirin Zearamane "making a huge breakfast on Sunday mornings with my best friend" by Paula W.

"a way of living joyfully" by Bob Boyle

"being blessed to own a successful business" by Deanna Fontes

"a lifestyle" by Sharon Saraga Walters

"an awareness that my choices create my life" by Gail Boenning

"being alive to experience my sorrows" by Manu Satsangi

"standing on the beach, feeling the gritty sand beneath my feet and between my toes, as the waves wash over them… and a gentle breeze whipping my hair around my face as the sun warms my cheeks" by Abigail Pierce

"a well of pixie dust that sprinkles itself on everything and turns the mundane into the meaningful" by Andy Chaleff

"living in peace and joy with what you have" by Scott Brining

"replacing please with thank you" by Nathan Davis

"recognizing all the good around me and staying true to it" by Noosha Ravaghi

"best expressed aloud" by Roy Schlegel

"noticing the beauty and wonder of the day" by Jayne Harrison

…

The various answers reflected people's perceptions beautifully. Each of these reveal some aspect of the concept, or the idea others have of the notion. It took me four decades to truly understand gratitude, and once I did, I knew with all my heart that I didn't want to live without it. My first encounter with gratitude took place, I believe, on my tenth birthday.

My parents threw me a little party. My dad set up a camcorder borrowed from the school where he taught. I sat at the head of the table, opposite the windows facing our backyard. Everyone happily sang happy birthday to me. Once the singing ended, I blew out the candles. A little later, I opened my presents, mostly clothes and objects which impressed me very little, not enough to make me happy. The frown on my face revealed my ingratitude. People who loved me had spent time and money celebrating me, all to make me feel special and loved, but this was totally lost on me at this young age in my life. I was a selfish child who just wanted toys. My dad recorded my birthday celebration. I don't remember this moment at all. I remember what happened after this moment, later in the day.

My dad told me to go into our television room and sit down. He then played the video of me during the party. I could see how I was acting. I could see my ingratitude. I could see the ugliness it radiated. My dad explained to me how mean I had been. He explained it and showed it to me. This created a memory I never forgot and never will.

Seeing yourself behave awfully is a powerful lesson. It's hard to watch and it takes a special person, a person who cares, to show it to you. My dad showed me a lot of love, tough love. I deserved to be punished, but, instead, he cared enough to show me the ugliness so that I could see the truth of the situation and make a choice not to be that person ever again.

My next encounter with gratitude, another powerful experience, took place in my teenage years. The summer after my freshman year of high school, I went on a mission trip to Jamaica with a youth group. We were there to build a house, but, for us teenagers, it was like a vacation on a tropical island for two weeks to have fun, gain new experiences, and build a house in the mountains. We hauled rocks and concrete up a hill that had to be over fifty yards to build the foundation. The next group would continue with the building. The man we were building the house for was a kind, hard-working Jamaican, who worked with us every day. He had a wife and a daughter. One day, he invited us all to his little home. His wife cooked for all of us. I was a picky eater at the time and didn't really like the food, but I knew that they didn't have any money and making this meal was their way of saying thanks, so I ate it all. Their efforts made me feel they really appreciated me for the work I'd done — a powerful demonstration of gratitude.

9

DEFINITION

"Every so often someone or something comes into your life that resets your focus. Rarely, however, do we know how profound these people, events, or experiences will be until we are far removed from them. They may be painful or joyful, terrifying or exhilarating, but what they all have in common is one core theme: When we look back on them, it is crystal clear that they have shaped us in ways that we needed to be shaped. They become the mile markers of our lives, defining the waypoints of our own personal journey, and yet, we likely never saw them coming, never asked or even knew to ask for them. And often they are so subtle and fleeting that we could have easily missed them if we hadn't paid attention for the split-second that they crossed our path." Thomas Koulopoulos

I met a lot of people during my gratitude journey and discussed whom and what they were grateful for. It's very easy to become fast friends with someone when you are speaking about gratitude and sharing personal stories about one's life. Each encounter and each story opened my eyes to a different aspect of gratitude.

At the beginning of my gratitude journey, when I wanted others to experience the feeling that I had received from writing the letter to my mom, I would seek out people posting anything and everything about gratitude on social media. If they were open to it, I would ask them to write a letter. I was all about letters back then. Letters were my gateway to sparking these moments of gratitude.

Kevin Caldwell, author and motivational speaker, was one of the people I connected with on Twitter. One day Kevin shot me a message with a link. It was a link to an Inc.com article titled "Do This for 30 Days and You Will Never Be the Same Again," by Thomas Koulopoulos. I read it and immediately wanted to meet the author because it helped me understand the true meaning of gratitude. It started with the promise that reading the story would be worth it and ended with "So, what are you waiting for?"... After reading his article, I was speechless. This guy got it, and, in his article, he had beautifully illustrated one of the best definitions of gratitude I'd ever come across. At that moment, more than anything, I wanted a letter from him.

I looked him up online and sent him a tweet that read: "A friend just shared your article on gratitude — really amazing stuff. Would you be open to collaborating on a gratitude project?" He messaged me back later that day, and that night we talked on the phone. Thomas became my friend, mentor, and savior in one instant. Years later, when I was working on *Dear Gratitude: An Anthology*, I asked Thomas to define gratitude for my book. Here's what he wrote:

"We talk about it all the time; we all know the word. We know the definition of gratitude, but I'm not sure we get it if we haven't truly

experienced it. Once you get gratitude, there is this aha moment, when you realize it's not just about thanking someone. It's about why you weren't already thanking them. What was standing in the way? What kind of deep-rooted issue did you have that created an obstacle to sharing that gratitude? If you answer that question honestly, then you'll get gratitude. You'll understand what it was about you that was flawed, that was broken, that was wounded, that prevented you from expressing your gratitude. Whatever it is that stands in the way is what you need to figure it out. Gratitude is a path to understanding and accepting yourself and your own power. Only then can you experience gratitude and share its benefits with others."

10

PRACTICE

The sooner we can understand gratitude and see all the gifts around us, the better. To be receiving so much and not taking notice of it is not healthy. In fact, it's a disease which directly affects our happiness. Its symptoms are a lack of appreciation for the gift of life, focusing on everything that is not going the way we want it to, expecting more than what we give, and failing to reciprocate the good we receive from others with our actions. Thankfully, this disease has a cure. The treatment requires some effort at first, but with some practice, it can change into a habit.

It's often said a good practice is to list three things we are grateful for every day. The idea is to take time, each day, to think about all the things and people we are grateful for in life.

The way to make things memorable and to create a more lasting impact is to list everything connected to the things we're grateful for as well. For instance, I am grateful for my coffee. I'm grateful for the water with which I make it, the beans, the machine in which I make it, the cup out of which I drink it, its warmth, and, after twenty minutes or so, the little perks the caffeine is going to give me.

Expressing gratitude in this way is much more powerful. It makes the person giving gratitude notice, more and more, all the things and people to be grateful for. It affects the giver of gratitude, the person it's for, and the audience. It intensifies it, adding another dimension to the initial expression of gratitude.

The idea is taking the simple statement of what we are grateful for and expanding it. It will make our appreciation grow. When we're grateful for objects, we can connect the people behind these objects. For instance, if we're grateful for a glass of water, why not take it one step further and appreciate where the glass came from and where the water came from. The origins of objects often refer to people. Someone made that glass, or maybe even someone gave us that glass. And the water?

I am grateful for water. I'm grateful I can drink it and use it in cooking, washing, and cleaning. I'm grateful that it flows endlessly into my home twenty-four hours a day, seven days a week. I'm grateful that somewhere out there people are checking the water and filtering out elements that would be harmful to me. I'm grateful that I was born in this day and age so I don't have to travel great distances by foot to a lake or a stream or a well to collect it. I'm grateful that I have easy access to it at all times.

Let's take it a step further, I am grateful that I get to pay the water company every month for this amazing service that really is worth far more than its cost to me. I love this incredible life-sustaining substance that flows endlessly within steps of where I lay my head. I can think of all the people and all the time it took to lay the pipes and how the creation of new types of metal made it safer. Then there's the filter cover on the sink, the adjustable volume and pressure, and the adaptable temperature.

This is wonderful to do when listing people we are grateful for in our life. For example, I am grateful for my dad. I'm not only grateful for my dad, but also for all the love, care, and support he has given me, for teaching me about love and dependability, for all the adventures and all the fun we've had together.

Naming what we're grateful for is the tip of the iceberg in relation to how amazing something or someone is and how much gratitude can be given. We can go really deep with the facets of every object and every person, starting with how we are connected to them, the reason for the connection, and how their presence affects our life.

11

MINDFULNESS

Many of our experiences exist because of countless others, and a little thought and mindfulness can show us each connection and give us the opportunity to appreciate it. Seeing the connections may need a little practice at first, and so does expressing gratitude.

Wendy Bett wrote a book titled *30 Days of Gratitude: Daily Gratitude Exercises to Uplift Your Thoughts and Improve Your Life*. In it, she provides exercises which, if done with consistency, can gradually eradicate the disease. I read this book and practice daily.

One of my first — and favorite — experiments was with color. More specifically, I had to make a conscious decision of what my favorite color is, then think of all the things that are in that color and are pleasing to me. Next, I simply had to go about my day, looking for that color. Every time I saw it, I just had to say *thank you*.

My favorite color, blue, appeared in many things around me. Looking for blue and expressing gratitude upon each discovery was an easy starting point. I ended up thinking about and seeing blue throughout my day and saying *thank you* to myself... for my watch band, someone's shirt, a car... Thank you. Thank you. Thank you.

This experiment is quite powerful because it brings us into the moment. The moment is where we want to be. Being present allows us to notice every breath and every element of nature. Gratitude is all about appreciating the present moment, appreciating what is here now.

Gratitude brings us into the present moment. It allows us to see each experience in a positive light. How? When we look for the good, that's what we find. Gratitude allows us to appreciate the things, people, opportunities, and privileges we have. Most of us take many aspects of our lives for granted: the nice comfortable space that is ours, the cool air on our face in a hot summer, the beverage that we enjoy, the piece of furniture we sit on. We forget that not everyone has these commodities, that we are blessed with these comforts. We only notice the good in a compare and contrast situation. We forget to appreciate these and, instead, turn our focus to what we lack and see it as a problem. We fail to look at problems as opportunities to learn a new method to achieve a task.

If where we are sitting is uncomfortable, we should be grateful we can feel this discomfort in our body and we should be grateful we have had more pleasant sitting experiences to compare this one to and realize it's not comfortable. If we are reading a book, we should be grateful that we live in a day and age where being educated and having access to books is taken for granted. I read all the time, and this sense of appreciation for this privilege of mine often completely escapes me. I'm grateful that I can read, that I've been educated to do this, that I have the freedom to do this, that I have access to books, and that someone wrote the books I read.

It may be difficult to notice how much we have if we are constantly surrounded by the people in our lives and the objects we use daily. If these are taken away from us, however, we quickly realize how much they had made our lives better, easier, and happier, and we miss them. For instance, we rarely notice or appreciate the air we breathe, and yet we only need seconds without it to realize how precious it is. Another example is our health. We don't normally focus on a tiny part of our body like a tooth until it aches and then we wish for the pain to go away. The longer we experience the pain, the more grateful we feel when it's gone.

There is so much to be grateful for every single moment that it would be impossible to name everything and everyone, but a general state of gratitude allows us to experience life's little reminders that come in the shape of negativity and pain as opportunities to appreciate all the good and express our gratitude.

12

CONTAGIOUS

Gratitude is contagious. It breeds gratitude. My gratitude for my mother led me to all the corners of this country seeking out others' gratitude in the hope that this gift would be seen. It's not hard to see. It's right in front of us. In fact, it's hard not to see it.

Unfortunately, as humans, we like to complicate what is truly simple. We overthink everything and don't realize how powerful our thoughts are. Our thoughts shape our ideas and beliefs, and these create the world we see. We focus on what we lack instead of all we have. We make choices that go against what is good for us. We choose not to take action. This is why a lot of people won't ever experience the true power of gratitude. The mind is amazing. At any given moment, we have the ability to choose what to focus on and determine what it all means, but our minds seem to have a negative bias. We can receive ninety-nine positive comments, but if one person says something negative, we focus on that one negative and give it so much power that it makes us forget the good; it makes us forget to be grateful. If there's truth in the negative comment, let's use it as an opportunity for self-improvement and be grateful for it. If there isn't, let's ignore it and focus on all things positive.

Let's live each day with a grateful heart. Let's take the time to say thank you. Let's look people in the eyes and appreciate however they are helping us move forward toward our goals. So many people help us out daily. Let's walk out with the mindset that we are going to truly thank one person every day. Let's express why we are grateful and why it matters to us. Let's share our gratitude. Let's make it shine so bright that it can allow others to see their gratitude.

Often, when something doesn't go the way we want it to, our first natural reaction is to get frustrated even though our mind is aware this won't solve any issue. In fact, it will take us both time and effort to undo that feeling and replace it with a positive or happy one. Having a different perspective will allow for positivity from the start. It may take some practice, but once it becomes a habit, we feel thankful and even excited for the situation instead of focusing on the inconvenience it brings us. It's important to always concentrate on the good; otherwise, we waste a gift, the gift of choice we've been given. We need to make time to appreciate our experiences and our ability to choose a perspective. Daniel Banfai, interviewed by Gratitude-Space Radio in 2020, said, "Busyness is the enemy of gratitude."

Our lives are made of moments and experiences. Each is either a prize or a lesson. Both are good, but we tend to see lessons in a negative light, maybe because they require some effort or present a challenge. My friend Rajesh Setty was the first person to share this idea with me in his Mindvalley Talk. He also talks about this in his book, Gratitude: Grow & Change Your World One Thank You at a Time.

In an interview on GratitudeSpace Radio, I asked Shawn Stevenson, the host of The Model Health Show, to define gratitude. He said, "I'm always looking for the gift in things, and when things are challenging, I am tuning back into the things I have to be grateful for right now, through this challenge, and that is what being grateful means to me." It's not the easiest thing to do, looking for gratitude when things are challenging. It's easy to be grateful for a prize. It's what I call easy gratitude. Being thankful for life's lessons is a bit more complex. We need to keep an open mind, expand our thinking, and remember that we are being taught something, and for that we must be grateful because it's a lesson that will serve us in some way, whether we know it at that moment or not.

"Gratitude is my shelter and suit of armor; the warmest wool, the softest cashmere, and the most satisfying feast. Gratitude is my compassionate and wise guide who will always point me to my True North." Margaret B. Moss

13

HOPE

We always have a choice to be either grateful or ungrateful. Living in gratitude allows us to know that we are enough and to be happy right now, as opposed to when some event happens. Gratitude is an abundance mindset. It shows us how rich we are in every way.

In times of uncertainty, when we are struggling or when we experience a loss, we may feel there isn't much to be grateful for, but, especially in those moments, gratitude can help. We can focus on the positive side of things by being grateful, or, as Lewis Howes said in a GratitudeSpace interview, by "being appreciative of what you DO have in your life instead of focusing on what you DON'T have."

When Noosha Ravaghi was in an impossible situation in her life, she chose gratitude. In her article titled "Gratitude & Hope" published in *Dear Gratitude: An Anthology*, she wrote that everything was taken away from her. "For seventy-three days, the number of days I was homeless, I listed everything I still had: I had a car: I could sit and sleep in it, it could take me to visit my dogs and to the part-time jobs I had left. I had a credit card: It allowed me to buy gas for the car and enough food for me to stay alive. I had a membership to the 24-hour gym: I could use the bathroom and shower day or night. I had clothes to wear: I could keep warm. I had my dogs' love: They were waiting for me to get things straightened out." She concluded that without gratitude she wouldn't be here today. "It was my constant appreciation for the little I had left that reminded me there was still hope."

In a GratitudeSpace interview, Shawn Anderson said, "Being grateful to me is never failing to look for the light…despite the dark."

As for me, I had to constantly remind myself of the magical power of gratitude and practice it, especially in those moments when my mother's absence felt unbearable, so that I could make the most out of the gift I'd been given, the gift of still being alive.

Gratitude has allowed me to see all the love in my life and appreciate all the things that continue to work in my favor. When something doesn't go according to plan, I remember it's not about getting everything I want; it's about appreciating everything I have.

I know that if I start each day thankful for the air I breathe and for a heart that keeps beating, I will be ready for whatever comes my way. I strive to keep gratitude always close and within my thoughts. I remind myself that I have all I need and so much more, that it has always been this way.

The secret is out: Gratitude works. Appreciating what you have will bring you into the present moment and, for that moment, you have enough. There is nothing wrong with wanting and working for more, but if you are coming from a place of ingratitude, once you achieve that next promotion, get that new car, or lose those pounds, you won't appreciate it.

"Happiness is a simple game of lost and found: Lose the things you take for granted, and you will feel great happiness once they are found." Richelle E. Goodrich

14

ENCOUNTERS

As a practitioner of gratitude for the past seven years, I can, without question, say that there are degrees to the practice of gratitude. I know this because I, myself, advanced a great deal in my practice, a direct result of my daily interactions, observations, and meditations. There are steps one must take in order to receive the full gift that gratitude has to offer. Just as a baby learns first to crawl, then gradually walk, and only then eventually run, there are degrees and levels to a gratitude practice.

In my first book, *Dear Gratitude: An Anthology*, I shared how the most profound form of gratitude was the gratitude that is initiated in another to share. I still, with all my heart, believe this to be true. I also know that it's not fair to expect a beginner or even a novice gratitude seeker to take this kind of action. That would be like looking at a one-month-old baby and yelling *run!* I'd be the mad man in the room if I expected anything to happen.

I told you about my first lesson in gratitude — or lack thereof — on my tenth birthday. Perhaps the second time I noticed gratitude was during my trip to Jamaica. Since then, my encounters with it have been very limited, or so it seemed. Now, decades later, upon reflection, I'm able to connect the dots, identify my experiences, and appreciate the complexity of it all.

Let me take you back to my grade school years when a teacher shared with us Maslow's hierarchy of needs. Our basic needs are physiological ones, which include air, water, food, shelter, sleep, clothing, and reproduction. Then we have safety needs, such as personal security, employment, resources, health, and property. Next is the need for love and belonging, which refers to friendship, intimacy, family, and a sense of connection. The next level up the pyramid has to do with esteem — respect, self-esteem, status, recognition, strength, and freedom. The highest level of the Maslow hierarchy of needs is self-actualization, or the desire to become the most that one can be. The teacher explained the pyramid and my young brain took this in, thought it made sense, and didn't really concern myself with it for another thirty years.

In 2020, I met a new friend named David Homan at a gratitude event, specifically at Chris Schembra's Gratitude and Pasta Zoom Dinners. Once he talked about his Orchestrated Connecting podcast and how he was trying to find the perfect questions to ask his guest, I knew that I had to check it out.

The next day I listened to his podcast on my outdoor run. The guest was Jenny Santi and she mentioned her book *The Giving Way to Happiness*. The breadcrumbs kept coming and now I wanted to have Jenny on my own podcast, GratitudeSpace

Radio, and I had to check out her book. I found her audiobook and started listening to it. Meanwhile, I set up a get-to-know-you call with David, and, a week later, chatted with him. I liked David's background in working with nonprofits and his mission in helping others. I told him about my own work and I mentioned that I loved his podcast with Jenny and that she sounded amazing. David said that he'd be happy to make an introduction and, later that day, connected me with Jenny.

A few days later Jenny and I met online. I shared that I'd love to have her on my podcast, and she kindly agreed. Now with a solid commitment from Jenny, I decided it would be best to read her physical book instead of listening to the audio-book. I ordered the book and read it as soon as I received it and enjoyed reading it. It's a great read for anyone who is into gratitude and kindness. It was in reading this book that I found out the real top of Maslow's pyramid wasn't self-actualization but self-transcendence. Of course, I jotted down many ideas, and these were the nuggets that I took into the interview with me.

In my mind's eye, I could see Maslow's pyramid transformed into a gratitude iceberg, where the tip was reflexive gratitude. The intent and emotion relating to gratitude were right below the surface. Finally, below those, was relational gratitude, where the connectedness of everything is felt. All the ice under the water, the whole of what is unseen, was catalyzing gratitude.

I then pivoted that idea to gratitude and, already holding Maslow's hierarchy in my head, I started talking about a hierarchy of gratitude. I'm not sure if she said it or I did, but Palmore's hierarchy of gratitude was conceived right there in my living room while talking to Jenny Santi.

I talked with my mentor, friend, and Inspirationalist Bobby Kountz, and set up a call with my old friend, gratitude brother, and mentor Thomas Koulopoulos to share the concept. After further discussion of the concept, I realized that what I was really describing was the mechanics of gratitude and not a hierarchy. After chatting with my mentors, I decided this was what I would work on.

15

ROADMAP

Ever since I started my gratitude journey, I'd been looking for ways to get other people involved. I asked them to write letters to their loved ones. I knew at the time it wasn't enough, but I didn't know what else to do. I shared everything in any way I could so that more and more people could feel the magic of gratitude the way I had. Then I interviewed people and many trusted me with whom they were grateful for. I made videos of interviews and posted them on my website to motivate others. That created a little buzz, but it wasn't what I wanted. I started writing daily and stating what I felt grateful for in a journal. After months of doing that, I met an editor who suggested constructing an anthology. I created *Dear Gratitude: An Anthology* and people from all over the world contributed by submitting their essays and letters. When the pandemic shook the world, I collected people's perspectives on their lessons learned, most of which expressed their gratitude, and made *Dear 2020: Letters to a Year That Changed Everything.*

Now I had come up with a gratitude roadmap, which I could share with the world so that anyone seeking a healthier life through gratitude could get an idea of what to do and where to go with it all, taking it step by step, reflecting upon it, and knowing that these practices take time to implement and digest — as any worthwhile practice would.

Everyone at any stage of their own gratitude journey can benefit from it. The more consistently a person practices it, the more they get from it. It's like going to the gym and working out consistently every day versus going to the gym and working out once a week. Which will create a better outcome? It's like Alan Cohen says:

"Gratitude, like faith, is a muscle. The more you use it, the stronger it grows, and the more power you have to use it on your behalf. If you do not practice gratefulness, its benefaction will go unnoticed, and your capacity to draw on its gifts will be diminished. To be grateful is to find blessings in everything. This is the most powerful attitude to adopt, for there are blessings in everything."

I've spent a considerable amount of time reflecting on the mechanics of gratitude, and, as I experienced and understood it, it can be categorized in terms of how it is learned, felt, and expressed. I've categorized gratitude as reflexive, intentional, emotional, relational, and catalyzing.

16

REFLEXIVE

The word *reflexive* here refers to a form of action. It's an adjective relating to what is performed as a reflex, without conscious thought. The image that might pop into your head when you hear the word *reflexive* or *reflex* is that of a doctor with his miniature hammer hitting someone's knee joint. What happens next is reflexive. The leg jumps up from the hit and then rests back in place. This happens involuntarily and with no help from the person being attended to by the doctor. Other examples of reflexive action are when the alarm is beeping in the morning and you turn it off, you see someone is right behind you so you hold the door open for them, you're driving and you hit the gas when the light turns green, or you say thank you to the person at the cash register checking your groceries. These are all actions done without conscious thought.

Here's a little story: Ted and Nancy are planning to take their daughter Samatha out on her first trick or treating experience on Halloween. Nancy takes three-year-old Samantha costume shopping, and Sam chooses a Princess Elsa costume from her favorite movie, Frozen. On October 31st, Mom helps Sam get into her costume and puts on a nice long dress and a long redhead wig and says she is Ariel from The Little Mermaid. Ted, sporting a nice brown suit and small wire-frame glasses, will be Sherlock Holmes, accompanying these two Disney princesses. The three head out together for a walk as Ted and Nancy teach their daughter the proper trick-or-treat etiquette. Right before they are to walk up to the first house, Nancy leans down to talk to Sam. "Sam, I need you to understand what's going to happen. Once we get to the door and ring the bell, someone is going to answer. When they do, we will all say 'Trick or Treat'. OK?" Sam nods. "Good," Nancy continues. "Now, what will happen next is they will give you candy, and what do we say when people give us things?" Sam thinks for a few seconds and says in a tone that's more of a question, "Thank you?" Nancy smiles. "That's right, my little princess. Let's go!"

This is just a parent teaching her child to say thank you. It's a lesson many parents teach their children in different ways. This is a good trait to teach children, but it's only half the story; it doesn't explain what is really happening. It's almost an exchange in action and not a personal thing.

I was raised to say *please* and *thank you*. When we are young, our minds can only understand so much, and this may be the extent of gratitude we learn at a young age. What is unfortunate is that when we get older and we can understand the mechanics of being grateful and sharing thanks, no one discusses it... and why would they? Many people have learned to automatically say *thank you* when someone does something for them. It's reflexive. Someone holds the door open for you, you say *thank you*. It's proper etiquette.

When saying thank you is an automatic reflex with no thought behind it, then it's reflexive gratitude or thanks. What if we stepped out of the unconscious reflexive state and acted with purpose and intention? Let's turn our reflexive gratitude into intentional gratitude.

17

INTENTIONAL

"Gratitude is a lens you see the world through which elevates your senses, your interactions, your entire life." Andy Chaleff

Most of us go through life without being fully present. One common example is our daily commute to and from work. We take the same streets, pass the same buildings, hit the same stop signs, and speed past the same green lights. We do all of it in a kind of fog. Essentially, we see and remember nothing. It's all the same, day in and day out — almost as if these trips were lost time.

A case from my own life that happens twice a week is my shopping experience. I pick up all my groceries and get to the register to have a person scan the items, bag them, and receive payment. I say thank you and leave the store. In most of my adult life, this all happened in a fog — a white noise experience. It happened all the time, and I would be in a reflexive state during the action. I'm sure it happens to many people very often.

During my gratitude journey, I decided I wanted to wake myself up from this reflexive state and experience life. I wanted to create memories and be present. To accomplish this, I decided — with intention — that I would pay more attention.

How did I pay more attention? By being present. It's that simple, really. Just a little attention to the moment we are in makes us present in that moment, gives our actions purpose, makes that moment count, and allows us to be mindful of everything around us. We begin to see more, notice more. We become aware of our surroundings and appreciate everything around us. A collection of these moments of presence is a day lived with intention.

One of the gratitude exercises I had learned at the beginning of my journey was to choose a color — I chose blue, my favorite color — and say thanks out loud every time I saw that color. That first day I practiced looking for blue things, my day became so memorable. I started making other changes in my routine just to get out of the fog of a mundane everyday experience. One day, I took a different route to work. Another, I counted the lights on the way. Achieving presence is simply accomplished with a little attention and makes everything feel fresh and new.

Ferris Bueller says: "Life moves pretty fast. If you don't stop and look around once in a while, you could miss it." This is how you stop and look around: by being observant, grateful, and vocal.

Every interaction matters. You never know what will manifest from your expression of gratitude, not only in your life but in a stranger's life. We never know what people are going through and what they are feeling, but all people want to feel seen and appreciated. By being present, appreciative, specific, and intentional, we create moments and memories. Creating intention in our gratitude takes practice, like anything else.

Back to my grocery store experience... I made a simple change to it. How? I was simply present in my moment — by not staring at my phone as the person rang me up, by looking around me and observing what was going on, by simply asking the person what was good that day, by smiling, and by looking at their name tag when thanking the cashier and using their name when expressing my appreciation for their help. Read that again: expressing appreciation for their help. The difference may be subtle, but saying why we thank someone changes the action and gives it intention.

I recently read a story someone posted on a social media platform that sums up being present. A professor who taught leadership at his university handed out the midterm exam, and it only had one question on it: What is the name of the lady who comes in here every day and empties the trash and cleans the boards? She wears her name on a badge pinned to her blouse. Only one student got the name correct; the rest complained about how unfair the test was. Then the professor told them the test was about how we treat the people who do things for us each day that we don't think are important. He then asked if anyone knew what the most important job in a hospital was. After answers such as the CEO and the owner, the professor responded by asking what would happen if the housekeeping staff decided not to come to work one day. The point was that the cleanliness of the hospital saved lives each day because housekeeping came to work each day.

That *why* adds a whole other level to the level of gratitude we feel and allows us to go down the rabbit hole of gratitude, and, trust me, this is a rabbit worth following.

18

EMOTION

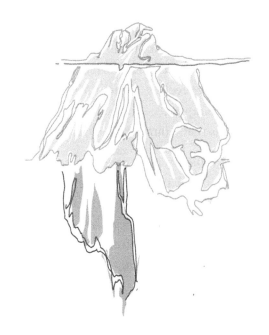

Very often, the *why* has to do with our senses and our emotions. Studies show that our senses and emotions are closely intertwined. For example, if we hear a fire alarm or smell smoke, we feel fear or at least that we're not safe. What we feel is often affected by our senses. What we see, hear, smell, taste, and touch can provide us with information on how to feel, and our senses play an integral part in our emotional processing, learning, and interpretation.

When we are children, we are taught to use our senses to investigate our surroundings. We rely on our five senses every day. They send messages through receptor cells to our brain. Our eyes translate light into images, our ears transform sound waves into signals, our skin's specialized receptors send touch signals, our nose is stimulated by chemicals in the air, and our tongue's taste buds send their own signals.

Whether we use one sense at a time or all five senses at once, each of them is linked to our brain, which figures out what the signals are and creates feelings, which provide insight, our six basic emotions — happiness, sadness, fear, disgust, anger, and surprise — which is really our entire experience of life.

For me, coffee is linked with a sense of energy and positive feelings. These feelings can be triggered in me from not just tasting coffee but also seeing a cup of coffee, smelling it, or even just hearing a coffee maker. Why am I grateful for my coffee? The smell of it when it's freshly brewed, the warmth it brings my belly, the energy it brings when I drink it.

Why am I grateful for my office chair? It was my mom's and I remember going to the office supply store to get it with her. Also, it's super soft and comfortable to sit in and its wheels are strong, which make it easy to pull in and out of my desk.

Why am I grateful for my father? He has loved me my entire life. He has a strong laugh, which I now find contagious and uplifting — although I will add that this same laugh used to embarrass me at the movie theater when I was a kid. He is a person I can always depend on.

This can even be done with people I have never met. For example, I'm grateful for the guy who invented the air conditioner because I'm sitting in my home right now, enjoying the comfortable cool air while it's hot outside and because I sleep peacefully and comfortably every night, and because my clothes are dry and fresh, not sweaty.

This can be done with anything and anyone. Our senses are associated with feelings and emotions, and what we are doing is remembering all the things we have to be grateful for that are right below the surface.

If we pay attention — with intention — to each of our experiences, we realize all of the things we enjoy have countless other things we are grateful for attached to them. As soon as we notice this, the world and our everyday existence will change.

∼

I was interviewing one of the authors of *The Book of Ichigo Ichie: The Art of Making the Most of Every Moment, the Japanese Way*, Hector Garcia, on GratitudeSpace Radio. The book is about not letting the moments of our lives slip away because every moment in life happens only once and is sacred.

I asked him how he'd explain gratitude to a ten-year-old. He paused, and I could tell he was really thinking. Then he essentially said gratitude is the moment that I change my focus from the one thing that is bothering me or that is wrong to realizing the ninety-nine things that are going right for me.

As human beings, we have only control over what we think, so let's make the most of it and focus on those senses that bring us all the positive emotions. Let's be thankful for those. Let's let emotional gratitude feed our heart, and our soul will never grow hungry again.

19

RELATION

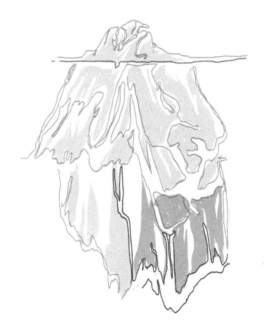

If you are sitting in a place where you are grateful and you love your life, you can then look back at everything that has happened — the good, the bad, and the ugly — and say it's ok.

It's ok because that had to happen so you could be the person you are in the present moment.

Relational gratitude is the appreciation of everything relating to a present situation for which we're grateful. What does it mean? I'll give you a true story to illustrate my point.

Corey is one of my best friends. I mentioned him at the beginning of this book. I originally met Corey when I was in elementary school. My parents went to a certain church, in which they made friends. The church had a program for kids. Corey and I met in that kids' program. Sometimes we spent time together outside of church. He has a memory that I don't hold of playing with a hula hoop in my parents' basement and playing Super Mario Bros 3. He was also at one of my earliest birthday parties at Lazer Blaze, which was the local laser tag place. I, again, don't have a memory of this, but photos from this party clearly show him there. Then we didn't see or talk to each other for six or seven years until I was fifteen or sixteen years old, and I started attending the same church's high-school weekly event called Vision. There Corey and I became reacquainted, but it was a hello type of thing once a week. I had the opportunity to go with this group to Panama Beach, Florida, for spring break, and this became the catalyst that allowed Corey and me to become better friends.

Today I'm grateful for Corey. What moments, choices, decisions, and situations in the past have caused this present gratitude? One was that my parents chose that particular church to go to. Then Corey and I interacted, and it might have been our parents getting together that caused that to happen. Again my parents had their hands in creating the possibility for this friendship to happen, and either our parents or we ourselves were close enough for him to come to my birthday party, creating a memory for him — Corey sure has a better memory than I do about all things. Then life happened and we didn't interact for years, but then I chose to start attending the weekly meetup called Vision. Then I got to go, with my parents' help and money, to spring break with the group, finally connecting with Corey on a deeper level with quality time spent that has projected us into today.

Today I'm grateful for not only Corey, but also all those causes that resulted in the effects, which, in turn, created new consequences to allow me to have Corey in my life today and be grateful for him. This is what I call relational gratitude.

There's something I sometimes wonder about. It's not the easiest question to ask, but, as painful as it is, it does cross my mind: *What things am I grateful for that have come directly out of my mother's death?*

The biggest lesson was that I value my life and the lives of those around me more. Nothing is more real than losing someone that you love the most. It's a hard lesson, but one that will forever change us in ways that we could never have on our own. It's a card that is dealt but one that no one would ever choose.

My relationship with my dad has changed. I loved him before, but my love for him is different now. There is a closeness that is present because we lost Mom. I stated before how my dad's pain put my pain in perspective. She was my mom, but to him she was his life. We are now like soldiers coming home from a great war. We have been changed, and no one else experienced or saw what we had together.

The direction of my life changed entirely. The message I posted on my mother's Facebook wall four months before her death made me see everything differently. It sent me on a journey I never expected to be on, and it made me pursue gratitude, which has made me find happiness.

Isn't that what all human beings are looking for? How can I not be grateful for what has led me to happiness?

20

CATALYZING

Loss allows us to see what we still have; it allows us to appreciate it. It brings perspective not only to our lives but also to the lives of others around us. Death is not a sentence, it's a gift. If life never ended, it wouldn't have any value. If you could, for all time, have breakfast with your best friend, it would lose its value and not be special. It's the fact that the world is unpredictable and in a state of entropy at all moments that allows gratitude to exist and makes every moment special and unique. It was when I lost my mom that I realized all I wanted was to be a catalyst for gratitude.

I came up with many ways to do just that: asking people to write letters of gratitude to share on my website, hosting gratitude events and capturing on video things people are grateful for, gratitude tours across the country asking people what they are grateful for and capturing those moments to share, interviewing people on GratitudeSpace Radio, collecting essays and letters on gratitude, *Dear Gratitude: An Anthology*, creating another anthology of people's perspectives during the pandemic, *Dear 2020: Letters to a Year That Changed Everything*, doing gratitude pop-ups during events, gratitude bombs, gratitude birthday parties, gratitude postcards, gratitude stickies, talking to people who were involved in spreading gratitude and kindness, etc.

Kindness, in all of its forms, is a massive catalyst for gratitude. This could be as simple as buying coffee for someone or being a volunteer at your local community center. Kindness is just being present with another human being and letting them know that they matter by simply putting your phone away and being with them, giving someone your attention, and letting them know that they are worth your time and focus.

But I don't just mean kindness to strangers or others. Kindness to yourself is a form of gratitude — kindness to yourself and loving yourself. Might I recommend writing a letter of gratitude to yourself? Love is an effective catalyst for gratitude and by choosing to love yourself, you will be more present and giving to others with your love and you will create a space for this love and kindness to come back.

The magic of being part of the creation of these spaces is that you will continue to have new memories filled with grateful moments. This will help you in those moments of uncertainty, those moments when you feel lost, when your feet are off the ground and everything seems out of control. In those moments, it's these memories and experiences that will help ground you and allow you to step out of the mess and come back to the realization that this is only a moment of your life.

To appreciate the highs, you have to feel the lows. If you have had someone cook for you all of your life, then you don't really understand and can't appreciate the skill, time, and love that it can take. Share in the cooking, cut up the vegetables, and go ahead and slice your finger accidentally because it's all part of the process. Appreciate every moment, and share your stories. Share all of it — the good, the bad, the ugly. All these parts make you who you are and change you to a new you. Every experience changes you. Every exchange teaches you something. Share it all.

The idea is to share gratitude. If it's not shared, it's not gratitude. Gratitude is meant to be given back. It's contagious, and unlike a virus, the more it gets spread, the better! The more spaces created to share it, the better. With intention and purpose, I have created thousands — literally, thousands — of conversations about gratitude with others, and each of these interactions has offered me a new perspective and allowed me to discover even more things to be grateful for.

Gratitude is a choice. This means that we all get to sit at the table regardless of our family background, shoe size, upbringing, favorite sports team, or how we like our coffee served.

Gratitude is also a habit. The amazing thing about any habit is the more you practice it, the easier it becomes. You can get so comfortable inside a habit that you will enter a flow state.

Be a catalyst. Share gratitude and let it spread.

THE 5 STAGES OF A GRATITUDE PRACTICE

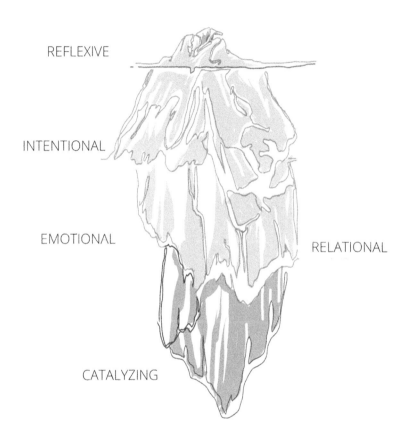

21

MINDSET

Gratitude begets gratitude, and I will continue to do this work regardless of whether I'm ever able to make a considerable living with my gratitude art. I've never really looked at it as work anyway; for me it's joy. There are those that would quit something if they could not find a way to monetize it. I will never quit on gratitude.

I now write in my gratitude journal that I am grateful for all the gifts the universe wants to give me. This mindset has really changed my life and showed me how rich I am in moments, memories, and friendships.

I didn't always feel like this. I had moments of uncertainty — many moments of uncertainty. It has taken a lot of practice and perseverance. Since my mother's death, I've wanted to share gratitude, and I did what I could, but I didn't know how to effectively share it.

I left my home in Louisville, Kentucky on April 22, 2016, to host Gratitude New York for what was supposed to be a twelve-day trip landing me back in Louisville on May 2nd. I would not arrive back home till over six months later, carrying the weight of the strongest depression that had ever taken residence in my mind and body.

I had high hopes, back in 2016, that a gratitude movement was about to start, that someone would see the work I was doing with all the space I was creating and would want to partner with me to create more spaces, that an angel investor would appear and give me the funds needed to start a gratitude movement. That didn't happen, but I never gave up, either.

Now, I have many people in my life who believe in this gratitude mission and will converse with me about all the ideas I have in creating these spaces. People whose retainers or hourly rates I could not afford to pay freely share moments and ideas within this gratitude space. People with amazing talent and love have entered my life and have helped me with my mission. I am who I am because of all my life events and choices.

Gratitude never sleeps; it doesn't hibernate; it is found in remembering and by looking for it intentionally; it is a practice. With fresh eyes, any day can be seen as a miracle. Albert Einstein stated, "There are two ways to live your life. One is as though nothing is a miracle. The other is as though everything is a miracle." I see everything in my life as a miracle. My whole existence is a miracle, from my grandfather surviving the second world war to my infant brother's death that led my parents to conceive me. My entire life is a gift, and everything around me is also a gift. My sharing these ideas with you is a gift. I hope this book helps you live your life as though everything is a miracle.

FOR FURTHER STUDY

I have read many books that have helped me in my journey. It would be impossible to list every book I've read, but I do want to share a few of these gems with you. I hope they will help you as well:

The Life-Changing Power of Gratitude: 7 Simple Exercises that will Change Your Life for the Better by Marc Reklau

The Book of Ichigo Ichie: The Art of Making the Most of Every Moment, the Japanese Way by Héctor García & Francesc Miralles

Thursday's Note by Sharon Saraga Walters

Thanks A Thousand: A Gratitude Journey by A. J. Jacobs

The Daily Stoic: 366 Meditations on Wisdom, Perseverance, and the Art of Living: Featuring new translations of Seneca, Epictetus, and Marcus Aurelius by Ryan Holiday

Man's Search for Meaning by Viktor E. Frankl

The End of Fear Itself: Simple Steps to Live with Courage in a World without Worry and Anxiety by Steve Bivans

Honeycake: Counting All My Blessings by Medea Kalantar

Begin with Yes: 10th Anniversary Edition by Paul S. Boynton

GRATITUDE CHECKLIST

To Rocío:

Thank you for being my wife, for loving me, and for continuing to make me laugh and smile daily. Thank you for being you. Thank you for moving from your beautiful home, family, and culture in Colombia to be with me in Louisville, Kentucky. You are the living embodiment of love, not with your words but with your actions.

To Thomas Koulopoulos and Bobby Kountz:

It sure is true that energy seeks out energy. Well, it's been a long ride and you both continue to play in the creative sandbox with me and, for that, I'm grateful. I envision a day when the three of us will be together in the real world, sharing gratitude. Thank you both for sharing gratitude out into the interwebs. I'm grateful that we have found each other… and, as they say, nothing has ever been the same.

To Paul Boynton:

Thanks for always being there to chat gratitude and for assisting me in sharing it! Thank you for the foreword to this book. Thank you for giving me the honor of an interview on GratitudeSpace Radio. Many thanks to the "Begin with Yes" community for participating in our collaborative efforts.

To Dad:

Dad, I love you so much! You continue to show up for me and support my vision of spreading gratitude across the planet. I am grateful for you. I think of you every morning and count myself blessed that you are around and that I can enjoy the ride on this big bowl of water floating in space with you.

ABOUT THE AUTHOR

Chris Palmore, The Gratitude Junkie, is the creator of *Dear Gratitude: An Anthology, Dear 2020: Letters to a Year That Changed Everything, and Gratitude Journey: Volume 1.* Chris is a gratitude conductor, coach, creator, and author. He is the founder of GratitudeSpace and a host on GratitudeSpace Radio. He has a Media and Performing Arts degree and a minor in Video and Broadcasting from Savannah College of Art and Design and is a proud member of the International Alliance of Theater and Stage Employees (IATSE). He lives with his wife, Rocío, in Louisville, KY.

ALSO BY CHRIS PALMORE

#1 New Release — amazon

CHRIS PALMORE

Dear Gratitude

AN ANTHOLOGY

"I'm so thankful for Chris Palmore. This book raised my serotonin level at least 30 percent. We need stories like these, especially now."
— A.J. Jacobs, *New York Times* Best Selling Author

CHRIS PALMORE

Dear 2020

LETTERS TO A YEAR THAT CHANGED EVERYTHING

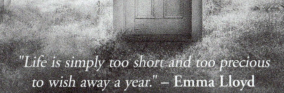

"Life is simply too short and too precious to wish away a year." – Emma Lloyd

Gratitude Journey

Volume 1

Made in the USA
Monee, IL
30 November 2022